STANFORD
WHITE

Stanford White
in Detail

Samuel G. White

Photographs by Jonathan Wallen

The Monacelli Press

For our granddaughters
Lucy, Eve, Abigail, and Jane

Photographs copyright © 2020 Jonathan Wallen
except p. 4 © Kristy May, p. 14–15 © James Ewing,
p. 43, 44–45 © Wadsworth Atheneum and Museum,
p. 46–47 © Ben White, p. 209 © Larry Lederman

Library of Congress Control Number: 2020937543
ISBN: 9781058935388

Design: Jena Sher Graphic Design
Printed in China

The Monacelli Press
65 Bleecker Street
New York, New York 10012

Contents

Introduction

Together with his partners, Charles Follen McKim and William Rutherford Mead, Stanford White led the most famous, and, at the time, the largest architectural firm in America. The two older architects were already running a small office when White joined them in 1879 to form McKim, Mead & White. Each of the partners brought a critical element to the initial arrangement. McKim's social connections would become major players in the world of business and culture. Mead's organizational abilities allowed the office to handle progressively larger projects, while Stanford White, whom Mead said "could draw like a house on fire," provided the spark.

Most of their early commissions were residential, and their designs for informal shingled dwellings captured the spirit of the age. Nearly one thousand commissions followed over the next thirty years as McKim, Mead & White transformed the appearance of American cities. Major projects included the Boston Public Library, Pennsylvania Station, Madison Square Garden, and campuses for NYU and Columbia University in New York, the Girard Trust in Philadelphia, interiors of the White House in Washington, D.C., and reconstruction of Thomas Jefferson's Rotunda at the University of Virginia. Their fame was not limited to the eastern seaboard. Twenty-five million visitors from around the world came to Chicago to see their work featured at the 1893 World's Columbian Exposition, and McKim was the first American to be awarded the gold medal of the Royal Institute of British Architects.

The success of McKim, Mead & White was due in part to their good fortune to practice at the cusp of post–Civil War prosperity, but it also reflected the value of extraordinary talent, appreciation for the best architecture of the past, and the combination of distinct but compatible artistic personalities. McKim was the leader and, together with White, the firm's principal designer. Educated at Harvard and the Ecole des Beaux-Arts in Paris, he was master of the axial plan and devoted to the architecture of ancient Rome, the Italian Renaissance, and eighteenth-century New England. White's apprenticeship with Henry Hobson Richardson provided a foundation in both practice and procedures, but it was his year in Europe in 1878–79 that gave him a taste for the picturesque complexity of medieval architecture. Mead graduated from Amherst and spent a year at the Accademia in Florence. Never a particularly gifted designer, his contribution to the firm was, by his own admission, to "keep his two partners from making damned fools of themselves."

If Mead could be remembered for his success in managing personalities, and McKim for his fidelity to solid forms and a severely classical idiom, nothing defines the work of Stanford White as much as his ornament. Few if any architects before or since could employ decorative motifs with such flair, draw on so great a range of ideas, or achieve a density bordering on saturation without losing control. The effects were dazzling, but the designs can be analyzed in more objective terms, starting with the sources of a decorative vocabulary that spanned from historic precedent to the product of a remarkable imagination.

Stanford White was a classical architect, and his career fits squarely in the 2,500-year classical tradition, but for him the orders were an opportunity rather than an end in themselves. Columns, entablatures, architraves, and pediments were blank canvases awaiting decorative treatment, an attitude that extended to virtually every other surface and feature. From the Greeks he borrowed strigilation, the tight repetition of s-curves based on the tracks of a comb, or strigil, with which Hellenic athletes scraped the oil off their bodies. For him ancient Rome meant the Pantheon, while Byzantium, the successor to the Holy Roman Empire, inspired his mosaics, with the more gold leaf the better. With its celebrations of all things beautiful, the Italian Renaissance became his lodestar and the source for so many of his ideas. He transformed palazzi into gentlemen's clubs and commercial buildings, filled his interiors with rare marbles, and covered every surface with swirling arabesques.

White's appetite for beauty respected no borders. He collected temple ornaments from Japan, carpets from Turkey, tiles from Holland, and mashrabia screens from Morocco. On a New England walking tour with his partners, he acquired a taste for the plain brick walls and delicate doorways of Federal houses, a subdued vocabulary that would appeal to his more self-assured clients.

As if the built world didn't offer enough, White looked to nature for inspiration. Representations of animals appear throughout his work from peacocks and bronze crabs to wrought-iron spiders in their webs—White did have a taste for the bizarre. Scallop shells abound, and carved fish scales cover everything from the frame of a gilded settee and the panels of a marble sarcophagus to the shingled interior of a chapel in a seaside resort. Plants appear as well, not only literal reproductions such as the woven cane of plaster ceilings or the foliate bases of his columns for Prospect Park but as the raw material for some of his most unusual choices, beginning with the split bamboo and mats of phragmites with which he covered the walls of his own country house.

It wasn't just the sources that make his work so distinctive; the range of materials and their treatment was remarkable. Ordinary wood furnished an encyclopedia of surface treatments and effects. The color and veining of the marbles he selected are designs in themselves, even providing the visual structure to his grandest interiors, but he could just as easily use pebbles gathered from the beach. Metal reveals the blows of a blacksmith's hammer as well as the delicate touch of the goldsmith. Ordinary bronze upholstery nails and carpet tacks are assembled into swirling patterns. Chunks of glass speak directly of the heat of the furnace, and leaded windows display the colors of the rainbow. Even the shards of broken beer bottles made it into White's designs.

White incorporated these materials into surfaces with intricate textures and patterns, often with a density approaching saturation, but he never let his ornament get out of hand. A fully loaded element—a strigilated frieze course, an enriched capital, or a door panel bursting with swirls of acanthus leaves— would be surrounded and literally relieved by walls or frames of plainer treatment. It is as if the saturated element could hold its breath no longer and was finally allowed to exhale. White's designs could breathe.

White was fearless in his juxtapositions. Japanese screens were placed next to Delft tile, Spanish ironwork, Louis XVI bergères, and—if the client could afford it— fifteenth-century tapestries. A house with elevations based on the Grand Trianon at Versailles has a stair based on the pulpit of a non-conformist meeting house in Newport. Unusual combinations of elements from vastly different cultures provided the most frequent opportunities, but White could also surprise with his choices of materials. His own house is covered with beach pebbles instead of clapboard, but the welcoming Dutch front door is flanked by delicate Federal-style side lites.

Stanford White's obsession with ornament and texture was a constant throughout his career, but his use of those elements over almost thirty years does reveal a trajectory. The earliest designs show him at his most energetic and imaginative, almost impatient; there is no room in some of the early houses for a single additional idea. He demonstrated a greater sense of balance in the work of his maturity, and yet the Whitneys' Venetian Room and the Madison Square Presbyterian Church, among his later creations, prove that he never lost the ability to turn up the volume to absolute maximum before turning it back down. And that silence could mean something. After a career as an ornamentalist, the sheer power of White's design ability in a restrained mode is nowhere more evident than in his last work, the Prison Ship Martyrs Monument in Brooklyn. The only ornament is the solitary lamp at the top of the monumental column, the only texture is the chaste fluting, and the only witnesses are four mute eagles. In his memorial to three thousand colonial soldiers who died in the holds of enemy vessels, the silence is deafening.

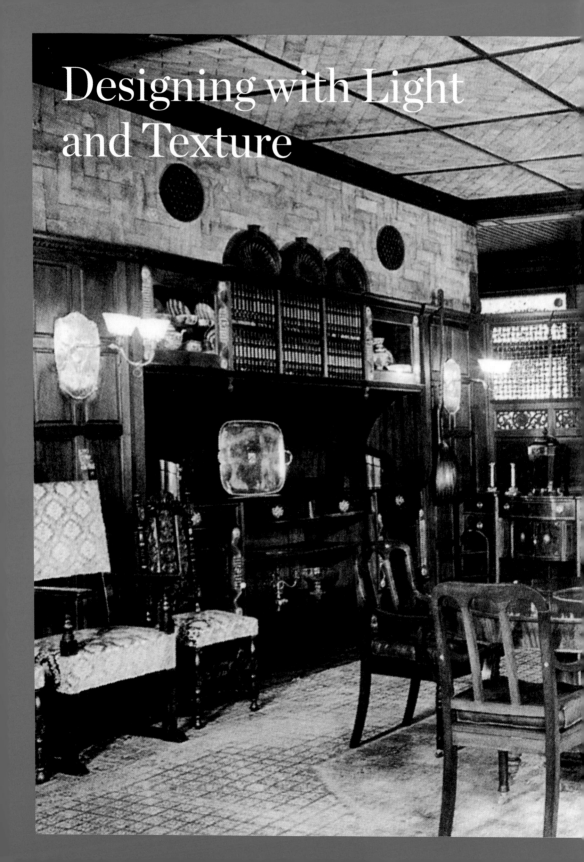

Designing with Light and Texture

Stanford White, c. 1880

Stanford White was obsessed with the play of light across textured surfaces, light that initially revealed their complexity and ultimately dissolved them in the wash of luminescence. While his contemporaries were recording the forms and styles of the past, White saw these precedents as armatures for expressing the energy and vitality of their surfaces.

White's interest in light, texture, and atmosphere over form, structure, and mass is evident in his earliest creations. Watercolors of the Hudson Valley capture the soft fog that diffuses the light and conceals the land forms framing the river. Drawings from his 1878 sabbatical reveal the same intangible atmosphere, but Europe introduced him to extraordinary—and highly tangible—buildings, and to record them White relied more on his pencil than his paint box. Those drawings reveal his fascination with the impact of strong northern light dissolving the complex surfaces of gargoyles, roofing tiles, and sash filled with tiny window panes.

What is first suggested in the sketchbooks of his European tour is confirmed in his work from the earliest designs. The glow of light from gas fixtures animates the basket-weave pattern of plaster ceilings as well as the woven bands of iron, sunbursts of rivet heads, and columns wrapped in chains that make the Veterans Rooms in New York's Seventh Regiment Armory one of the most remarkable interiors in America. Sunlight caresses the pebbledash cladding, fluted columns, and patterned frieze of his own house, Box Hill, while the same light penetrates the interiors to unlock the ornamental potential of unusual materials—from ceilings finished with cork or fish netting to walls covered with split bamboo or marsh grass. An underlying structure emerges from walls of Delft tile or white marble organized according to nearly imperceptible tonal variations. Slight surface variations in glazed terra-cotta animate the main stair in Box Hill as well as the facades of Rosecliff and the Ferncliff Casino. Light coming from two directions contrasts the delicacy of Federal-style doorways with the deep shadows of lattice, a combination that punctuates the rambling plan of James Breese's Orchard by transforming simple connectors into outdoor rooms.

Some of White's designs displayed their greatest effect in more subdued, but more luxurious settings. He created frames based on generous applications of gold leaf over shimmering layers of texture that complete paintings by William Merritt Chase, Thomas Dewing, and other Gilded Age artists. The same gold leaf covers a settee for Anne Cheney, on which densely twisting forms are juxtaposed against a frieze of tiny fish scales, one of White's favorite motifs. A gold necklace for his wife, Bessie, features a crab grasping a baroque pearl in its claws, recalling a similar creature with which he co-signed his first independent design for the base of the Farragut Monument in New York's Madison Square.

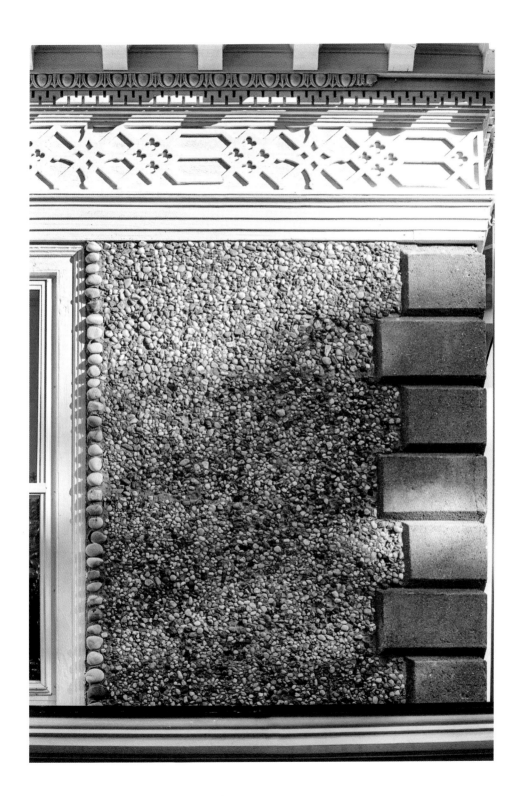

23

27

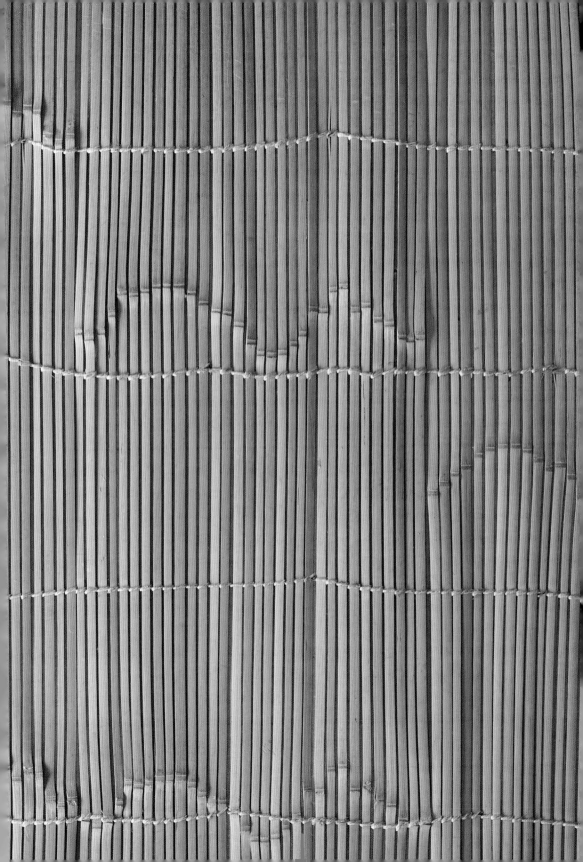

Inventing a Vocabulary

Stanford White, c. 1883

I n the 1880s, Stanford White and his colleagues responded to the increased opportunities for leisure in post–Civil War America with a new architecture that transformed the resorts along the East Coast. An amalgam of medieval French, English Queen Anne, and eighteenth-century New England precedents, this idiom was characterized by the architects themselves as "modern colonial," particularly in its reliance on gable roofs, multi-pane double-hung windows, and discrete classical moldings. Notwithstanding individual precedents, there was nothing revivalist about the work as a whole. In assessing it a century later, noted architectural historian Vincent Scully coined the term "shingle style," describing the houses as "the architecture of the American summer."

In parallel to the style's formal characteristics, White introduced a level of effervescence and energy to the details, as well as a taste for fearless juxtapositions that remain unique in American architecture. The repose of the Short Hills Casino is destabilized by its asymmetrical, nearly weightless entry porch and the surprising unwrapping of the tower's shingled skin. Medallions of beach pebbles and broken glass, a signature of White's early work, are set against waves of scalloped shingles in the Newport Casino and houses for Samuel Tilton, Percy Alden, and Robert Goelet. Slender columns of faux bamboo and lithe sea monsters support the weight of Isaac Bell's wrap-around porch, while Percy Alden's muscular tower terminates in a calligraphic flourish of metal wire.

White's interiors are even more innovative, revealing an unbounded, almost limitless imagination. A kaleidoscope of images is connected by a reliance on densely patterned surface textures, unexpected plays of light, shifts of scale, or unusual context. Wood is carved, chased, and polished in every possible direction. For the front hall of Isaac Bell's Newport house, White fashioned a fireplace alcove out of a medieval French bed, backing the open rosettes with silver foil to create an unexpected source of light. The walls around the stair are clad in over-scaled beaded board, while the walls and ceilings of the dining room are covered in woven cane, with the perforated lids of colonial bed warming pans added for punctuation. The fronts of sideboards are covered in swirling arabesques of tiny upholstery tacks, while hardware, light fixtures, and stained glass in exotic patterns evoke opium-scented passages of Arabian nights. For White, every surface was an opportunity, and few opportunities were neglected.

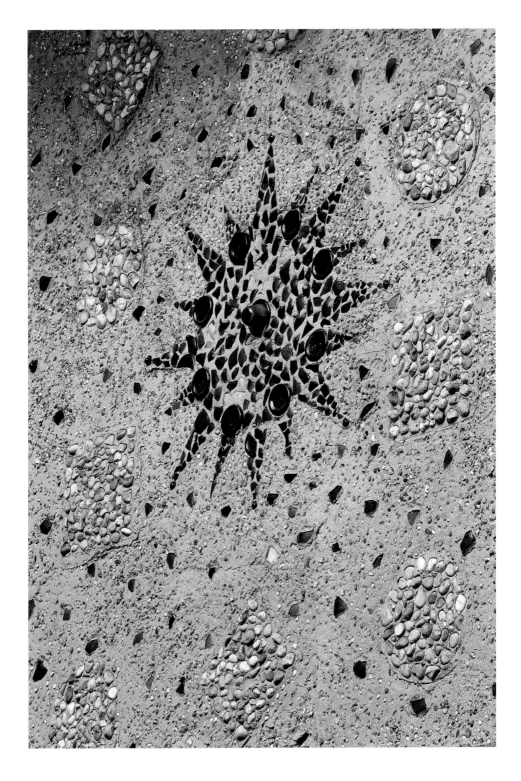

96

First Formal

Stanford White, c. 1885

By the mid-1880s, architectural patrons eager to demonstrate their wealth and sophistication caused a shift in the paradigm of the "summer cottage" toward a more formal expression. In Newport, that trend is clearly seen in Stanford White's house for Robert Goelet, a design that stretched the vocabulary of the shingle style to its limits, and in his additions for William Watts Sherman and David H. King, both of whom wanted to keep pace with Newport's emergence as a summer capital for high society.

Townhouse designs in New York, Boston, and Baltimore demonstrated a parallel development, reinforced by the inherently greater formality of an urban setting and the greater willingness of clients to spend more on their city residences. Henry Villard's rooms imply chamber music and high tea, while the massive three-family mansion for Charles Lewis Tiffany conveys a message of bedrock stability, belying the phantasmagoria of Louis Comfort Tiffany's apartment below the roofline. But the imposition of social discipline that accompanied these commissions resulted an expansion—rather than a limitation—of White's imagination. With new access to greater resources, he produced riotous combinations of materials and details and mutations of classical elements that seemed without precedent, resulting in a degree of opulence that was sometimes overwhelming but never overbearing. The fireplace in the front hall of Ross Winans's Baltimore townhouse simply explodes with color, while his office safe is sheltered behind a blazing emblem of brass upholstery tacks. Watts Sherman's drawing room marries Gilded Age opulence to cartesian discipline. Every house has a magnificent staircase, none more so than the Garrett-Jacobs spiral ascent to a Tiffany dome. Densely ornamented and highly finished surfaces enrich John Forrester Andrew's interiors on Commonwealth Avenue in Boston, but whatever White realized in varnished mahogany for Andrew, he surpassed for Henry Villard on Madison Avenue in New York. A clock designed by White with bronze zodiac figures by Augustus Saint-Gaudens emerges from the rare Siena marble walls of the staircase. Further upstairs that marble is carved into heavily embroidered balusters and spirited capitals with upturned volutes. But the stair does not stand apart from the rest of the interiors. Chunks of stained glass illuminate the vestibule, mosaics cover the floors, tiny nail heads transform the faces of doors into damask, gold leaf covers the vaulted ceiling of the Music Room. Neither the client nor his architect could restrain themselves or each other, and the effect is breathtaking.

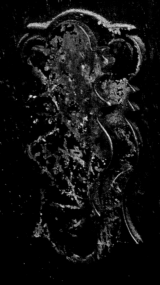

139

143

Experiments

Stanford White, c. 1895

The wave of post–Civil War prosperity generated new building types and institutional programs that were unprecedented in, if not unique to America. Challenges for Stanford White included churches to accommodate a pedagogical agenda as well as a spiritual mission such as Baltimore's Lovely Lane and New York's Judson Memorial; Madison Square Garden, an entertainment complex with multiple performance spaces that presented opera on one night, boxing on another; a monumental electrical generating plant for the Interboro Rapid Transit Company; the Bowery Savings Bank, an institution that used architecture to attract and reassure a thrifty clientele; and gentlemen's clubs for which the character and aspirations of their memberships were reflected in their elevations. Nearly everything White designed was, at some level, an experiment.

To meet the challenge, White employed new materials, new combinations, and new ways of looking at precedents, frequently drawing on European architecture to provide the framework for a solution. The economies of molded terra-cotta ornament allowed him to respect the investors' budget while presenting the IRT station as a Renaissance palace and to give the Century Association a facade that suggested the spirited intellectual and artistic activities within. The Herald Building, one of White's best and most original designs, was an ingenious merging of the Torre Orologica in St. Mark's Square with Verona's Loggia degli Consiglii, but the design also acknowledged the commercial function of the building with windows under the arcade overlooking the pressroom in the basement. Similarly, the new Tiffany & Co. headquarters was realized as a white marble Venetian palazzo combining muscularity with perfect proportions, while incorporating large show windows for display at street level and industrial steel sash to light the interiors of the modern office building above.

While the interiors of the early houses showed White doing a lot with a little, renovations of two churches demonstrate his virtuosity with expensive materials and his sure hand in combining them. The Church of the Ascension was transformed by a liberal use of Siena marble, mosaics by Maitland Armstrong, bas-relief angels by Louis Saint-Gaudens, and a monumental mural by John La Farge. At St. Paul the Apostle, he tamed the cavernous interior with a majestic half-domed ciborium covered with gilded mosaics that recall the magical interiors of Byzantium.

·MDCC

At the Top of His Game

Portrait of Stanford White, Ellen Emmet Rand, c. 1904

S tanford White was not responsible for the shift in taste toward the classical in the 1890s, but his contributions in that vein were so striking and so memorable that his mature work will be forever identified as the embodiment of the period. And those designs were not simply elaborate—they were beautiful. They radiate energy as well as balance while combining saturation with restraint.

From 1890 on, America's wealthiest citizens were demanding White's talents, and he was extremely productive. There are multiple examples to illustrate is maturity; four of his existing buildings—three residences and one institutional project—can represent the level he was able to achieve.

Payne Whitney was the scion of two of America's richest families. As a wedding present, his uncle Oliver Payne gave him a blank check to build a house on Fifth Avenue. White designed a forty-foot wide palace clad in granite, featuring allegories of fertility, a fountain ringed by columns of rare marble and incorporating an early Michelangelo, and the Venetian Room, a gilded and mirrored confection whose elaborate decoration explores a middle ground between architecture and furniture; it is one of his most original and most beautiful creations.

John Jacob Astor asked White for a pavilion to house the male bachelor guests at his house parties and accommodate an indoor tennis court, America's first indoor swimming pool, two squash courts, and a ballroom. The casino's elevations, based on the arches and pairs of columns of the Grand Trianon at Versailles, were finished in white glazed terra-cotta. The interiors were completely original. The main hall combines French tasseled capitals, Federal-style transoms, and a ceiling that recalls in plaster the cornucopia of fruits and flowers of an Italian Renaissance frame surrounding a Della Robbia Madonna.

Heiress to the Comstock Lode and one of America's richest women, Tessie Oelrichs wanted a setting for the best party in Newport's crowded social season, and White delivered a masterpiece. Rosecliff's exterior, clad in softly glazed white terra-cotta, transforms the Grand Trianon into a two-story residence with a cornice line punctuated by posturing putti, while the interior features Newport's largest ballroom and the most beautiful staircase in America.

Helen Gould was as wealthy as any of White's clients, but her ambitions would be realized in a university library rather than a house. The overall form Gould Memorial Library is based as much on Jefferson's Rotunda in Charlottesville as it was on the Pantheon, but the details are original to White. They range from the scalloped copper shingles that animate the surface of the dome to the saturated passages of copper cheneau outlining the projecting gables, the hyper energy of both relieved by smooth walls of limestone and the soft blending of roman brick. The interiors combine Irish marble columns and Tiffany glass and mosaics, surmounted by a coffered, gilded plaster dome that is a tour-de-force of applied geometry.

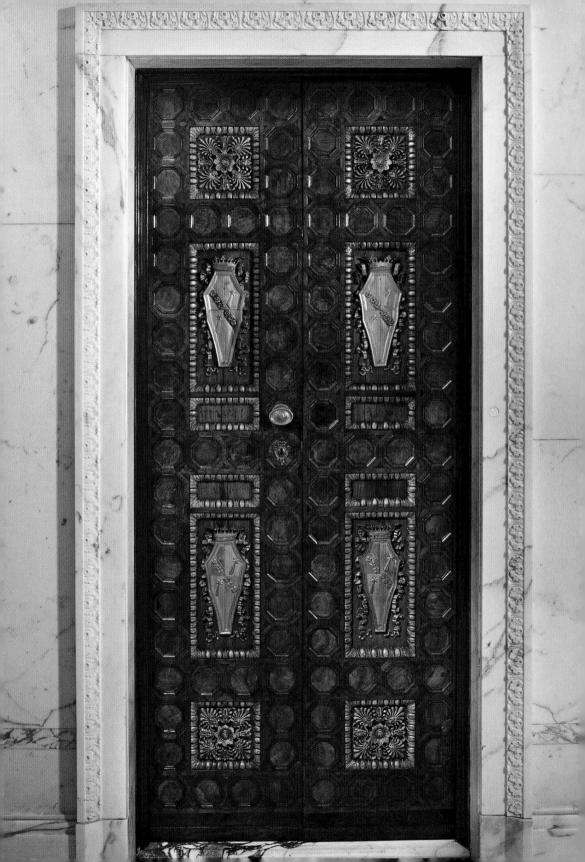

233

240

Captions

10–11 **Kingscote**
Newport, Rhode Island
1881

14–15 **Veterans Room**
Seventh Regiment Armory
New York, New York
1880

16–17 **Library**
Seventh Regiment Armory
New York, New York
1880

18–19 **Box Hill**
Saint James, New York
1892 et seq.

20 **Library**
Seventh Regiment Armory
New York, New York
1880

21 **Veterans Room**
Seventh Regiment Armory
New York, New York
1880

22–23 **Box Hill**
Saint James, New York
1892 et seq.

24–25 **Box Hill**
Saint James, New York
1892 et seq.

26–27 **European sketches**
1878/79

28–29 Box Hill
Saint James, New York
1892 et seq.

30–31 Box Hill
Saint James, New York
1892 et seq.

32–33 Box Hill
Saint James, New York
1892 et seq.

34–35 Box Hill
Saint James, New York
1892 et seq.

36–37 Box Hill
Saint James, New York
1892 et seq.

38–39 Box Hill
Saint James, New York
1892 et seq.

40 Gilded picture frame
c. 1890

41 Memorial to Joseph Morrill Wells
with Augustus Saint-Gaudens
1890
Oak Grove Cemetery
Medford, Massachusetts

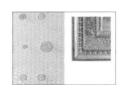

42 Library
Seventh Regiment Armory
New York, New York
1880

43 Gilded picture frame for Thomas Dewing's *The Days*
c. 1886

44–45 Settee designed for Anne Cheney
c. 1885

46–47 Box Hill
Saint James, New York
1892 et seq.

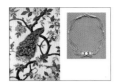

48 **Box Hill**
Saint James, New York
1892 et seq.

49 **Crab necklace
designed for Bessie White**
c. 1884

50–51 **Admiral David
Glascow Farragut
Monument**
New York, New York
1880

52–53 **Box Hill**
Saint James, New York
1892 et seq.

54 **Wedding portrait
of Bessie White**
Augustus Saint-Gaudens
Frame by Stanford White
1884

55 **The Orchard**
Southampton, New York
1898 et seq.

56–57 **Short Hills Casino**
Short Hills, New Jersey
1880

60–61 **Isaac Bell house**
Newport, Rhode Island
1883

62–63 **Newport Casino**
Newport, Rhode Island
1880

64 **Newport Casino**
Newport, Rhode Island
1880

65 **Isaac Bell house**
Newport, Rhode Island
1883

66–67 **Ochre Point**
Newport, Rhode Island
1884

68 **Alden Villa**
Cornwall, Pennsylvania
1884

69 **Henry G. de Forest
house**
Montauk Point, New York
1882

70–71 Alfred M. Hoyt house
Montauk Point, New York
1883

72 Isaac Bell house
Newport, Rhode Island
1883

73 Alden Villa
Cornwall, Pennsylvania
1884

74 Isaac Bell house
Newport, Rhode Island
1883

75 Alden Villa
Cornwall, Pennsylvania
1884

76 Samuel Tilton house
Newport, Rhode Island
1882

77 Ochre Point
Newport, Rhode Island
1884

78–79 Newport Casino Theater
Newport, Rhode Island
1881

80 Isaac Bell house
Newport, Rhode Island
1880

81 Newport Casino
Newport, Rhode Island
1880

82 Alden Villa
Cornwall, Pennsylvania
1884

83 Isaac Bell house
Newport, Rhode Island
1883

84 Newport Casino Theater
Newport, Rhode Island
1881

85 Quogue Episcopal Church
with Sidney V. Stratton
Quogue, New York
1884

86–87 Isaac Bell house
Newport, Rhode Island
1883

88–89 Alden Villa
Cornwall, Pennsylvania
1884

90 **Ochre Point**
Newport, Rhode Island
1884

91 **Samuel Tilton house**
Newport, Rhode Island
1882

92–93 **Henry G. de Forest house**
Montauk Point, New York

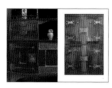

94 **Isaac Bell house**
Newport, Rhode Island
1883

95 **Samuel Tilton house**
Newport, Rhode Island
1882

96–97 **Alden Villa**
Cornwall, Pennsylvania
1884

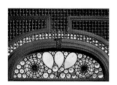

98–99 **Alden Villa**
Cornwall, Pennsylvania
1884

100 **Alden Villa**
Cornwall, Pennsylvania
1884

101 **Samuel Tilton house**
Newport, Rhode Island
1882

102 **Ochre Point**
Newport, Rhode Island
1884

103 **Isaac Bell house**
Newport, Rhode Island
1883

104 **Alden Villa**
Cornwall, Pennsylvania
1884

105 **Samuel Tilton house**
Newport, Rhode Island
1882

106–107 **Isaac Bell house**
Newport, Rhode Island
1883

108 **Alden Villa**
Cornwall, Pennsylvania
1884

109 **Isaac Bell house**
Newport, Rhode Island
1883

110 **Alden Villa**
Cornwall, Pennsylvania
1884

111 **Isaac Bell house**
Newport, Rhode Island
1883

112–113 **Charles Lewis Tiffany house**
New York, New York
1885

116 **John Forrester Andrew house**
Boston, Massachusetts
1886

117 **John Work Garrett house**
Baltimore, Maryland
1886

118–119 **John Work Garrett house**
Baltimore, Maryland
1886

120–121 **Kingscote**
Newport, Rhode Island
1881

122–123 **Kingscote**
Newport, Rhode Island
1881

124–125 **Kingscote**
Newport, Rhode Island
1881

126 **Henry Villard house**
New York, New York
1885

127 **Ophir Farm**
Purchase, New York
1893
Originally in the
Henry Villard house

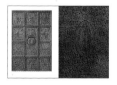

128–129 **Henry Villard house**
New York, New York
1885

130 **Naumkeag**
Stockbridge,
Massachusetts
1887

131 **Zodiac Clock**
Augustus Saint-Gaudens
Henry Villard house
New York, New York
1885

132　**William Watts Sherman house**
Newport, Rhode Island
1881

133　**Henry Villard house**
New York, New York
1885

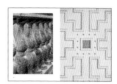

134　**Henry Villard house**
New York, New York
1885

135　**William Watts Sherman house**
Newport, Rhode Island
1881

136–137　**William Watts Sherman house**
Newport, Rhode Island
1881

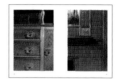

138–139　**Ross R. Winans house**
Baltimore, Maryland
1883

140　**Ross R. Winans house**
Baltimore, Maryland
1883

141　**Henry Villard house**
New York, New York
1885

142　**John Work Garrett house**
Baltimore, Maryland
1886

143　**Henry Villard house**
New York, New York
1885

144　**Villard Houses**
New York, New York
1885

145　**Ross R. Winans house**
Baltimore, Maryland
1883

146–147　**New York Herald Building**
New York, New York
1895

150–151　**Players Club**
New York, New York
1889

152　**Players Club**
New York, New York
1889

153　**Saint Paul the Apostle**
New York, New York
1890

154–155 **Church of the Ascension**
New York, New York
1888

156 **New York Life Insurance Company**
Kansas City, Missouri
1890

157 **Bowery Savings Bank**
New York, New York
1895

158–159 **Church of the Ascension**
New York, New York
1888

160 **Naumkeag**
Stockbridge, Massachusetts
1887

161 **New York Life Insurance Company**
Kansas City, Missouri
1890

162–163 **Lovely Lane United Methodist Church**
Baltimore, Maryland
1887

164 **Lovely Lane United Methodist Church**
Baltimore, Maryland
1887

165 **Century Association**
New York, New York
1891

166–167 **Ionic capital from Madison Square Garden**
New York, New York
1891

168 **Century Association**
New York, New York
1889

169 **Colony Club**
New York, New York
1908

170–171 **Tiffany & Company**
New York, New York
1906

172 **Tiffany & Company**
New York, New York
1906

173 **Prospect Park**
Brooklyn, New York
1895 et seq.

174–175 **Interborough Rapid Transit Company**
New York, New York
1904

176 **Prospect Park**
Brooklyn, New York
1895 et seq.

177 **Judson Memorial Church**
New York, New York
1893

178 **Judson Memorial Church**
New York, New York
1893

179 **Naumkeag**
Stockbridge, Massachusetts
1887

180 **Saint Paul's Church**
Stockbridge, Massachusetts
1885

181 **Goelet Building**
New York, New York
1887

182 **Cable Building**
New York, New York
1894

183 **Century Association**
New York, New York
1889

184–185 **Century Association**
New York, New York
1889

186–187 **Century Association**
New York, New York
1889

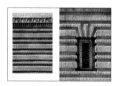

188–189 **Interborough Rapid Transit Company**
New York, New York
1904

190–191 **Payne Whitney house**
New York, New York
1909

194–195 **Ferncliff Casino**
Rhinebeck, New York
1904

196 **Rosecliff**
Newport, Rhode Island
1902

197 **Charles Dana Gibson house**
New York, New York
1903

198–199 **Payne Whitney house**
New York, New York
1909

200 **Rosecliff**
Newport, Rhode Island
1902

201 **Ferncliff Casino**
Rhinebeck, New York
1904

202–203 **Payne Whitney house**
New York, New York
1909

204 **Metropolitan Club**
New York, New York
1894

205 **Ferncliff Casino**
Rhinebeck, New York
1904

206–207 **Gould Memorial Library**
Bronx, New York
1903

208 **Ferncliff Casino**
Rhinebeck, New York
1904

209 **Gould Memorial Library**
Bronx, New York
1903

210 **Metropolitan Club**
New York, New York
1894

211 **Gould Memorial Library**
Bronx, New York
1903

212–213 **Ferncliff Casino**
Rhinebeck, New York
1904

214 **Rosecliff**
Newport, Rhode Island
1902

215 **Ferncliff Casino**
Rhinebeck, New York
1904

216–217 **Payne Whitney house**
New York, New York
1909

218–219 **Payne Whitney house**
New York, New York
1909

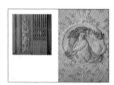

220 **Joseph Pulitzer house**
New York, New York
1903

221 **Payne Whitney house**
New York, New York
1909

222 **Rosecliff**
Newport, Rhode Island
1902

223 **Robert Wilson Patterson house**
Washington, D.C.
1903

224 **Ogden Mills house**
Staatsburg, New York
1897

225 **Payne Whitney house**
New York, New York
1909

226–227 **Ferncliff Casino**
Rhinecliff, New York
1904

228 **Prison Ship Martyrs Monument**
Brooklyn, New York
1909

229 **Gould Memorial Library**
Bronx, New York
1903

230–231 **Gould Memorial Library**
Bronx, New York
1903

232 **Robert Wilson Patterson house**
Washington, D.C.
1903

233 **Rosecliff**
Newport, Rhode Island
1902

234–235 **Hall of Fame of Great Americans**
Bronx, New York
1901

236 **Rosecliff**
Newport, Rhode Island
1902

237 **Robert Wilson Patterson house**
Washington, D.C.
1903

238–239 **Washington Memorial Arch**
New York, New York
1892

240 **Washington Memorial Arch**
New York, New York
1892

241 **Harmonie Club**
New York, New York
1907

242–243 **Stuyvesant Fish house**
New York, New York
1900